Graft

Publication of this book was made possible
by a generous grant from the Greenwall Fund
of The Academy of American Poets.

graft

POEMS BY

glori SIMMONS

Published by Truman State University Press, Kirksville, MO 63501
http://tsup.truman.edu

Printed in the United States of America

Library of Congress Cataloging-in-Publication Data

Simmons, Glori, 1966–
    Graft : poems / by Glori Simmons.
        p. cm. — (New odyssey series)
    ISBN 1-931112-03-7 (alk. paper)
    I. Title. II. Series.

PS3619.I559 G73 2001
811'.6—dc21   2001055533

Cover art: "Les Mains Libres," Ryerson & Burnham Libraries, Mary Reynolds Collection, © The Art Institute of Chicago. All Rights Reserved.
Cover design: Teresa Wheeler
Printed by: Jostens
Body text: ITC Legacy Serif 10/15. Display type: ITC Legacy Serif 14/15

∞The paper in this publication meets or exceeds the minimum requirements of the American National Standard—Permanence of Paper for Printed Library Materials, ANSI Z39.48 (1984).

For my parents
&
for Michael

Contents

Acknowledgments

Grateful acknowledgment to the editors of the following journals in which versions of these poems first appeared:

The Beloit Poetry Journal: "Against Nature" and "The Bookbinder"
Black Warrior Review: "Markings"
Controlled Burn: "Lexicon"
Cutbank: "Pomona" and "The woman smoothing her son's bangs"
Fourteen Hills: "Brown" and "It was the time of waterbeds…"
Graven Images: A Journal of Culture, Law, and the Sacred: "The Virgins of Murano"
Green Mountains Review: "Sometimes our lovers come back to us…"
New Millennium Writing: "The Lady of Oplontis Receives a CAT Scan"
Passages North: "Second Hand"
Quarterly West: "Hand mit Ringen"
Rattle: "Our Butoh"
Salt Hill: untitled
The Seattle Review: "Worn Jacket and Levant"
Southern Poetry Review: "The woman smoothing her son's bangs"

"Luena Fields" received the Poetry Society of America 2000 Lucille Medwick Memorial Award. Selections from this collection also received the Poetry Society of America 2001 Alice Fay Di Castagnola Award.

"Brown" was used in a short film of the same title by Michael Wilson.

My sincerest appreciation goes to the Academy of American Poets, Poetry Society of America, and Meader Family for their recognition and generosity; the Ragdale Foundation, Blue Mountain Center, and Villa Montalvo for the gift of time; and the University of Michigan and University of San Francisco for their resources and support. I would also like to extend my gratitude to the friends who have read and commented on this manuscript, especially Paula McLain, as well as to the teachers who have offered their guidance to me: David Baker, Alice Fulton, Lawrence Goldstein, the late Bill Matthews, OyamO, and Richard Tillinghast among others. My final thank you goes to Nancy Rediger and Truman State University Press.

The sign on the unlatched gate did not bid enter.
You say unfaithful. I say asylum, circling the white picket,
fingering a cracked plate, sentencing my pear slices.

Tonight, I charcoal my eyes & trespass
through the orchard, because I have someplace to go
& see no reason to tie on the beaten wives' shoes

& step from the night waning. As you follow,
listening for the string to undo me, I'll speak of tree limbs
striking the simple ground, a corset stripped

of its stays. If the trees are full, I'll pick the fruit,
and solicit your knife for paring. If you
lick the juice from the blade, do not say I fed you.

I

In the myth of childhood, we are orphans
searching for a riverbed to sleep upon.
Our hands sweep the ground, divining.

Autogeography, Sonogram Study

You will remember none
of this: the sound
torch's startle

as I exposed
your cuticle
in the river of blood.

I was the key
unlocking Lascaux's
cave, sunlight

curling
the page. My cacophony
discerned you

ghost lit
among my crime's 256
shades of gray:

apron
pocket, courtesan
fan, lampshade.

Already
I was
disappointed.

You revealed
the knowledge—
I will trade river

stone for atrium,
for glass. The rock
landing inside the house.

Your spine led
away
from me.

I followed.

POMONA

This is me crawling back, child of cold linoleum and haystacks.
By headlight, my father hurled your blonde bales
To buy the carburetor and gas as my mother bulged and studied biology.

You were never the perfect bride—
Too often you tasted of barn loft cider.
Too often your pruning lessened the seasonal gods.

I went to church every Sunday for you,
The smell of stove fire in my hair.

City where the white Ford stalled,
City of children reaching for cereal boxes from shopping carts,
City of forked roads,

There is a rental house lodged in my heart, a Shepherd
On a short tether, sheets hovering over lawns of lopped dandelions—
Their milky stalks.

In your lap I memorized the scripture of my hands
And learned to kick the dog.

You are the myth left behind:
A green suitcase, the Siamese slinking into my crib,
The .45 hidden between mattresses, safety unlocked.

From the porch an old woman reinvents the lie to marry you off
As a girl in the distance cries behind laundry lines.
In your prodigal orchards there are no birds.

The people migrate from your acred hands
In rusted trucks headed north.

Second Hand

We slide our hands along hangered gowns to shoulder pads,
    an embroidered rose, sequins sewn
in a moonlit room on another continent. Two red foxes,
    glass-eyed, chase each other
around a camel-hair neckline as you seek the lace, the wasp

    waists and unpack words we seldom use:
chiffon, raw silk, Angora. Some would call this excess *clutter*.
    Each accessory a hint to the crime:
jade cuff link, crooked hat pin. A herring-bone gabardine
    speaks the practicality of Hepburn,

Parkette tucked behind her pageboy ear. The maiden name
    sewn into the Navy uniform proves
the owner once here now gone, lost like change through
    the hinged fray of a Dresden clutch.
Among the pleats and darts, the mole-shaped cigarette burns,

    we search for the girls we might
have been. *Oh, Johnny.* You Bacall from under a fedora's
    felt brim for a Vaseline-smeared lens.
The distant scent of *Shalimar*, the sign of a woman of intention:
    pill box, veil, vintage smile.

IT WAS THE TIME OF WATERBEDS ...

and neighborhoods off the highway
named Camelot, the split
entry. *Passion bruises, love bites*
were just a few of our precious
euphemisms strewn across
backseats with coolers, camisoles
and *Sweetie, please. Not yet.*
Sunshine Sherry, the weather girl,
was off the air in the aftermath
of serial rape and copycat crimes.
The Real One stuffed an oven mitt
in his pocket, his neck branded by
the diamond kiss of an iron.
We called this *he-deserved-it,*
the devil's sign and learned to forecast
the rustle of lilacs. In the darkroom,
the yearbook advisor introduced
his own technique for straining
light—*use your girlfriends' tights,*
guys. It was he who discovered us
training for 10Ks bare-backs exposed
and didn't expose us. On Friday
nights, we raced our mothers' voices
down the downy paths we called
love trails. Grapple and noise.
"Keep the door open, please."
We didn't. We were learning too fast,
our boyfriends' hands leading ours
past the concave fairways beneath
the fly, beyond hard-on to ever
after: *Please. Sweetie. Please.*

Sometimes our lovers come back to us

As we enter by bus the cracked empires of dust bowl towns

The Stargaze Motel's red arrow
Casting a lipstick blotch across the window
A blush across the highway

As we ride through that blush
A cowboy nodding off on our shoulders
We feel them getting closer

Pulling back the curtains in their cul-de-sacs
Taking the corsage from the refrigerator

Remember their fragrant shaking hands
The silver tipped pins

Baker's son
Adopted one

Nervous in the pitch-black of country road turnoffs
And cineplex alleys

Sometimes as we mouth
A wretch like me
Below our mother's sweet octave

And the minister who covered our noses with cloth to dunk us
Opens his arms to the congregation

The one with bloodshot eyes
The one with dainty hands

Taps on the stained glass
Dangling a lost earring
Reciting our crumpled words back to us in porch-light interrogation

Sometimes grown
Sometimes unchanged our lovers return

Freckle counter
Exhibitionist
Their various comforts

To guide us slowly through museums
The back streets of our arms

Remember their wrists against our hems

The woman smoothing her son's bangs

looks young against the Dakota snow.
Her dad's a bird man, she tells me,

when a pheasant jumps a post.
She misses it—the town
where her father's mayor and taxidermist,

where there's not much use
in whispering, the church secretary
leaving casseroles in your mailbox

with bad news. Behind her, the furrow
where sky and field meet
is little more than a suggestion

like the nod that says I'm listening
or the house without door
her son has outlined on the train window.

Out there her ex feeds kindling
to a needy wood stove,
warming a room for a girl

who wears thermals and slippers most days,
so quiet when she enters a room
he doesn't even notice her.

His white-sided house stands invisible
in these wintered plains that give up
only game tracks, a thin vein of barbed wire.

Poor Leda

What little water flows there must be poison.
Years she avoids roadkill, the eyes
little bargains, unspoken pleas. At the gate

the turkeys circle her like the lonely souls
of highway migrants, a salesman's speculative smile.
Each peck an annunciation—

she's sure she carries the leader of flightless birds.
In her confined time, walking more with a waddle,
she nurses the homely fowl now fenced in

and fattening. They funnel her milk like empathy
until she bleeds into the always autumn grass.
In the two-fisted season of barely enough

and slaughtered flocks a son is born:
lucky penny, spring flowing from granite, the basket
where all her eggs are stored. He is unmarked

and precious as a groom except for a brown patch
on his arm, curdled as her cold nipple,
where a wing might have grown in a less frugal land.

MARKINGS

I.

Each birth notches a woman's pelvis like a belt,
the skeleton
a hinged cradle splitting.
Whether the child is born dead
or crying, a mother carries it with her
like a cedar's rings.

2.

The incision where doctors cut the tumor, budding
like an irritated tongue,
from the man's cheek
healed into a narrow seam,
a closed mouth, a story
with no teller.

3.

The male skeleton grows rough
like an antler,
the female smooth as horn.
His body marked time   like a prisoner: the iamb
of heartbeat, the ache of midlife a life sentence,
the broken vessels of drink
speeding across the nose.

4.

He lost the tips of two fingers sizing cupboards,
no noticeable gashes,
only open air
and misshapen fingernails.
Still, his fingers found the trigger
and aimed for the scar.

WESTERN DIVIDE

At the end of the porched year
point us toward sepia lands
county fair still lives clad in chaps
& calico. Revolver in lap.

Deliver bonnets to cover
our short hair & aproned dresses
we can tie on over our pants.
We promise to smile

without blink for the duration
forgiving our fathers
their cat calls
the butchered beasts.

Grant us sun when the hay lies
cut in the field & the men prepare
to leave the house to reap
the rocky soil to fill our mouths.

Often they return to the wrong chairs.
Remind us then of our own trespasses
into unpromised hands
as the others slip into our half-dresses

our half smiles to walk steadfast
beside our fathers to cross the divide.
Hallowed be the dose of truth
small enough to swallow.

Lead us back to the oak mantle
the one-room house
its draped doorways
where we learned to make love quietly.

LEXICON

And for several years, my lexicon—was my only companion.
—Emily Dickinson, 1862

Walls. What she made of them.

Through the window, a garden
cast in snow. Beneath the frozen ground

December loses its dull edge, bulbs
unfold like words in white space.

Each blindfolded bud keeping watch. Alone,
she finds relief in the familiar terrain

of paper. Her questions do not seek proof
of what could have been, but simply of God:

what spring makes of snow. The passersby toss
a stone at her window, pay a silver dollar

for her capitalized words, leather bound
and legitimate as a family tree—

each tongue-tied leaf a lexicon.
In the wall behind her desk, spins a globe:

a feathered pen, an ear
spilling ink, the metaphysical.

Through her paper garden, a window.
An open window.

AGAINST NATURE

> *i.*

The third way of grafting—

Go to a smooth apple or pear in April
When the trees get liquor

& seek a branch
Which has green eyes of less than a finger.

& tear it from the tree.

(Notes from *The Expert Gardener*, 1640)

I am forgetting the liquor of my female body. Once I poured it into pear
contours, starched bowls, lighting my face red. Now I plant it inside an
architecture of trellis and trouser. Reshaping my form like an old woman who
separates her toes with cotton—toes refigured by a century of pointed boots.

What narrow roads did she balance herself upon? What hills did she climb?

She will become small in the end, the scar of light that ripples across walls
and wakes the awake. She is the molecule in the pill that teaches my body to
take its new wooden shape.

Pear.

In the lover's hand, a pear.
In the hysteric's hand, a pear.
In the Virgin's hand, sometimes a pear beside the angel and olive leaf.
Beside the son.

We've named them Bartlett and d'Anjou—
names that speak of the incision of their limbs and the healing that followed.
The perfect cut and lace of two opposites to make it right.

They've taken on lovers' names, fathers' names, the botanists' names.
The fruit reminds me of running until I could not breathe among the leaves.
The pear in my father's hand was a trophy.

ii.

(The grafts have been named as well,
determined by
the cut, the angle, the union.)

I am searching for a silent place, a quiet stretch of skin with no sex mark—
the stomach flesh that pulls to bandage burned limbs or form a penis where
there was none.

In a hillside orchard, a girl water fills each moat. Sun freckles her back,
tightening the flesh around her bones. She becomes more than fair, other
than girl.

Not knowing which fruit will bulge from the random blossoms, she reads
their tags—their latinate titles—to speak to them. They become what she
calls them.

This is not a dream. It is the end
of the French dynasty,
a foggy morning

and a woman's husband is her malady.
She hides his list beneath
her cloak to step

from the convent room
for what he calls *her idiotic ramblings.*
His request: a prune-colored redingote,

salmon pate, madeleines.
And a dildo
of dark mahogany,

waxed smooth as a child's arm.
The more real, the better,
he tells her. *Test it in your mouth.*

Margaret on men.

When I touched the male body, it felt wooden.
Like a puppet, the fingers were pinned to fold.

The torso was a tailor's mannequin draped in white oak.
They lay across my body like sleep.

Mostly I closed my eyes.

iii.

The fourth way of grafting is—

How buds are transported
& bound upon another tree
Like a plaster is tied

To a man's body:
This sort of grafting is called
In Latin *Emplastrum*.

Always the old woman's deformed toes brought me to ask: *what is perfection?*

I imagine how my body would feel if I could touch it once as a stranger or a god; if I could touch it as male: my cheek, my thigh. *In what form*, I ask myself.

Still life.

A pine table set inside Rembrandt black.
Someone has left unexpectedly, spilling the silver platter
of fruit. The candle almost burned out.

The lives are still illuminated:
a grape cluster, trout's head, dewy mum.
And two pears.

One standing, the other on its beckoning side.
The knife blade just there.
The pear reflects the shades of Holland's

deciduous regions, a late bruise—
the tint of wound and repair. Cold lips.
I am searching for a silent place.

Myself on dressing.

Sometimes when I pour myself
into the fabric, I spill.

This is my other self:

a nude woman
dancing in front of a window.

I desire her.

iv.

(Cleft graft,
whip graft, bud graft.

They are names of beauty marks,
small tattoos—

games played in dominance
and submission.)

The Marquis finds so many reasons
to slap her cherry tart face.
Still she returns

with the key to her room,
her orifice. Mythology's
sad helper, she is a tattered book

to be read with one hand,
her pain a dog-eared
placeholder at love's core.

She delivers gifts
to fulfill him in his prince's cell,
his stone turret.

My body will become a house
Margaret cannot enter.

I will lie beside her
like a puppet she cannot move.

I love her body beside mine,
yet not mine beside hers.

In the orchard, the girl folds up her sleeves, takes off her boots, freeing her ripening toes. She runs her lips along her arms, sucking in the warmth of her cheeks like a hard kiss. She calls herself Boy.

v.

How apples & other fruits are made red—

If you graft upon a wild stump
Put the sprouts in Pike's blood prior.

The mahogany stalk
was once a single tree
in a Rouen field.

Then the ax came down
to cut it into a gentle thumb.
The carpenter polished it

into a smooth root.
She understands its thirst,
its hollowed vein

that could contain a map.
She is the ridiculous shopper
scarf covering her basket of bounty.

The Marquis, writing that
the stoic holder
is once again too narrow

for his continents,
will accuse her of spending
too much on herself.

I will take from the inner thigh, hip, abdomen and wrap my skin around itself, grooming it into a new limb, ordering doctors to do what nature did not. I will wake inside my father's trophy form.

The garden.

So often I return to the garden, the orchard tree
and stand beneath it.

A woman is offering up a fruit
botanists have yet to name, painters have yet to paint.

Does it have thick, pocked skin or is it varnished smooth—
what trees would you graft to create the forbidden?

I am searching for a silent place.

II

THE BOOKBINDER
Mary Louise Reynolds, 1881–1951

WORN JACKET & LEVANT
14. rue Hallé, 1950

All that was left—her personal effects,
               her words—Marcel unbound
     & burned,

      leaving behind only the bindings:
                  copper-spined coffins,
           backdoors

with teacup handles & green glassine.
          Alone on street corners, Marcel
     searched

      for a reminder of her, thread
                 to hold the fray. In his hands,
         a hollow-backed casing

encased in black. Along the streets,
        only the slam of shop shutters
     ring clear, in tact.

FOOTNOTE
Minneapolis, 1901

As a girl, I danced as I undressed,
    loosening my sash and shoelaces,
        stringing them like leaves behind.

Even then I was contained,
    girl in organza collecting laundry
        from the line, bare feet drenched

in dew—beneath moon glow,
    my nightgown was a scrim.
        My legs delighted in their innocent

transgression, captive's dance.
    In my hands, each sheet seemed
        a contraband letter, survival skill.

SELF-PORTRAIT OF A MATE
Greenwich Village, 1918

Beloved Matthew, what cool ground
does my letter find you moling through today?

Your whisper is a rip in New York's swelter.
A jar of sun tea browns on the window ledge.

Its sepia dissolve is time passing slowly.
We are not a matched set, earrings

slandering the ear, but a shell that hums
the perfect pitch. Not two gloves

on separate hands, but one, split
at the seam, waiting for the needle's mend.

Until you return, I'll drink the tea alone,
cool my cheeks with the glass sweat.

    Your Mary.

ONION SKIN & SPINE
Paris, 1920

She maps his death in the unhinged streets—
                 door knockers,
      watch face, no hands,
           finding comfort

in the tangible. Her husband's cough
               returns in the turning
        of *Tribunes* at cafe tables.
            The stones of Montparnasse

cool her hands, the rain confuses. With scraps
               she seams
        his body's symmetry.
            Stab sewn, tightly laced.

Her needle plunges through his starched layers
               to collar, tie,
        waistcoat, shirt.
            A Greenwich Village efficiency.

Undershirt. Vacant bed in the corner.
               Each book cover
        the meeting
            of two hands. Skin.

MANIFESTO FOR THE HANDS
To Marcel, Pre-occupied France, 1927

My old goat lover,
Satyr Face,

I miss our half nights.
Lately you starve me

at the chess table,
your fingers sweet

with the burlesque bouquets
you've plucked from the streets—

still asleep in your bed.
With you, I master

the art of less
handling, entering the sheets

like a tomb. Eyes closed,
feeling for a way out.

In Cafe Dôme I doze off,
wineglass in hand.

Found objects, play things,
attractions of the mere physical variety,

you say, forgetting I salvage
everything. On our first full night,

your moan was the sob
of my dead husband,

who mourned not my betrayal,
but his own.

If I offered my hand,
who would take it?

Mornings I wake to solitude
replenished, my skin cold

as a statue under snow.
Feral Love, today you've served me

the worst no,
mistaking another bride.

Cela n'a pas d'importance.
You hand me

these condolences like pennies
to place over my eyes.

For the thaw, I'll let go three
times over. For you,

Marcel. For Matthew.
For myself.

—M.L.R.

Signature
14. rue Hallé, 1939

On the corner of *rue Hallé*, I spot
the half-shell of a broken compact,
its cheek empty of rouge. I spare

its possibility, add a window
to a calfskin door, a puff
to seduce the serif words which wake

like a music box as I open the newly
bound book.
In my *atelier*, I fashion a veneer

from lizard screens, goat skins
softened in vats by human feet.
The feet, too, subject to bind.

Skin inside the skin of another.
Patent, pointed, refined.
For Cocteau, I stencil stars

on the endpapers, discreetly lining
the covers like lingerie.
Inside each crease, my hands trace

the tree's sacrifice—bark grain, leaf,
Daphne entrapped in laurel.
Nymph who dared refuse

Apollo's hold. With a knife, I split
each signature along its folds,
unsentence the page. The words

are free to be chased again.

       For *Le Surmale*, I clip morocco

into Monarch wing, secure a corset stay.

GENTLE
Occupied France, 1942

When they send the composer away,
     the alley quiets
  to one cart's cobbled plucking.
She salvages what she can—

   old spectacles, wigs,
     blurred passport photos. She resists.
  Answers only to *Gentle*, binding the living
     in garments of the dead,

  plucking stars from coat sleeves,
nailing francs into shoe heels.
    After so much scrapping of landscapes
     & last minutes, she doesn't open the door.

  Visitors come the way of dead hornets.
     She resists.
  Refusing to answer the farewells
from Marcel's New York.

  No one understands
    the *ruliere's* need to shut herself
  from the world. When Marseille's red tiles
    warn no,

  the Pyrénées open to pages
of snow. With Man Ray's *Lips*
    rolled in paper like a gypsy babe,
     she walks away from the light.

  They charm the skies. The stars suggest
     an earlier Paris that falls
  toward her, a staircase
descending from wax threads. She resists.

Endpapers

No interest (age).—Major S.W. Little, Office of Strategic Services, 1944

Dear Sirs:

My application states the following—
    brown, gray, 53 years gone by. To this you add:

Sorry, no bronze wings, no special detail today,
    ma'am. I'm intimate with no's hollow meaning,

its take away. Under its fact, New York grows
    simple & small. I frequent empty like a café.

Go away gentle, Mary, you taunt, forgetting
    I have resisted more. There is nothing else.

This limp is a buried limb beneath the Spanish snow.
    Still I arrived. Officer Small, I've memorized

your answer by heart & know well how to pick
    its lock. Sincerely yours, Gentle Mary

Body Valise
American Hospital, Neuilly, France, 1950

This knot inside me is my undoing,
a key locked in baggage.

It's here in the Minotaur's drawer, tucked among
toad skins, roses dried & quartered.

I'm familiar with the Lady Thing—
its deckle-edge,
its double entendre.

No invitations, it just arrived.

Like arias in radiators,
armies pouring across borders.
Like forgiveness.

Drink still keeps me warm.

I'm well over the times you left me,
sugar cube solid on my spoon "to puzzle the chessboard"
& more, Marcel.

The maps you papered
to the walls still allow us our lonely,
but the studio is a yellowing heir.

Now you'll be the widow, My Colophon.

Keep the boxes & casings together.
Burn my private things.

III

The windshield, the windshield wipers
then the rain—reminding the glass
that it, too, is a slow liquid.

Time Capsule

At the open window: rooftops like overturned books.
Siren howls. The orange resting on the table
reminds us of the sun, growing closer
and more apologetic each day.

Mornings we tuck our dread into undergarments
and water the cat. His face is like a clock,
my eyes like olive pits. At twilight I feed him my garlic skin;
he washes his plate to show he is thankful.

There is no altar, no contract.
With the scraps of his silence, I mend my own.
Lately we stray from the television's
absinthe glow into the rain.

Our Butoh

Each night we

(wakeful webs   my straight jacket
unstrung   your fly
slightly open)

do what we can

(I talcum my toes   you slip into
your sinew & we come
crawling)

to forget

(the moon weave's dated preface   seductions
of sap-soaked boxes
& narcissus)

what we know about

(this pillowed dune   dust settled on bedposts
our loom's   threadbare
seal)

the body.

FOUL, *600*

France, on the announcement that pleasure during sex is sinful

I have lost him today:

my bleached man, wringer of hands, Gregory.
Even now he washes himself of me.
We kneeled close to the mosaic to muffle ourselves.
The turquoise garden held a lapis shepherd,

held a goat. We climbed its crown of fence,
I wore its stones. He opened his tunic
& I did not look back, but kissed his hands,
thinking them a gift. Quickly he pulled them

from my lips into his sleeve as if they were severed
by my sin. He feared himself, walked to the well.
From the pulpit, he speaks of ill in the church—lust
tucked in the communion cloth like chewed gristle.

Touch is foul. The saint is speaking of this ram's mouth.
I am aware of my tailbone riding the pew,
my threadbare wrists, the herd dog's panting tongue.
I am aware of being fed by his immaculate hand.

Chronic

If I fall while dressing the plank of your back,
I will not be clad in nurse white, humming

noon's remedy, my fingerprints insignificant rings
about your neck. Leech-hearted, I have found

little comfort in the giving of comfort.
An aloe leaf is a blade when drained.

I would gladly trade this pox-veil
for scale & fin, defy the salted waters & breathe

it all in like the Iron Lung in a freak show.
The body can't promise to serve its master.

You know that. The cyclopsed fish rides the current
toward the dam despite its one eye to shore.

What would it take to entice you to stay
a little longer, ignore the bedsores surfacing

solemn as beggars' hands? We could accumulate
your ailments like properties, line the terrace

with their lion-maned lanterns, present them
on silver platters like Catherine's eyes.

Together, we could breed a new strain of invalids
beneath the nitrous sky. So before I fall,

Consumptive Love, unsnap the respirator
& unbandage your thighs. I will let you suffer.

Rehearsing Death

The castor wheels pigeons hobble on
are the cities we wore beneath our clothes:
scolding lights, raspy corridors. Once a waltz,
my feet pinched inside my shoes the factory's distance.
Your lungs were brown bags spilling
their stingy inheritance—mine shaft minus
coal. My arms: drapes
blown out beneath the window.

I divvy up the linens corseting this chamber
into Grethel's pinafore: an asterisk,
a cloud, any roadside cross to guide
our bodies back. Listen. Can you hear the Liars
dipping their quills? The redhead will strap me
into wings in which I hug myself.
Sweetheart, come I morse into my palms.
I hear your breath just on the other side of the cloth.

CLOUDS, *1677*
Holland, on the discovery of sperm

Love is pure science tonight—

Anton has come to me thrice, kissing me
fewer times, before lifting himself
from the horsehair. Beneath the microscope
his fluids are moving. I agree by definition—

all liquid takes on the form of its containment.
I remember the stillborn in my most silent winter.
He came out in the shape of my sorrow. Anton's
smudge reminds me of the skim that spread

across my mother's eyes. Gradually, I was lost
to her, a child crying beneath the ice.
I will not be surprised if Anton finds life
in his milk—I have tasted it & it tastes of tears.

We are all cloud & precipitation. Is that not good science?
Through his glass, he shows me that stagnant waters
hold living creatures. Perhaps we all are descendants
of the canals swimming toward earth on our bellies.

Plank

Nijo Castle, Kyoto, known for its nightingale floorboards that warn of intruders

A traveler turns to let a stranger pass
Coat covert black   suitcase spilling

She crosses a medieval   narrow passage
White nest   not unlike her own

Here is the locked gate   the splintered rail
Tree that fits in her palm

This is the board that is quail
This is the board that is cockatiel

Once courtesans scissors-stepped these floors
To wake samurai to bird call

This is the leaf pinned into her hair
These are the sleeves in which she hid her hands

Do not step where he hates the song
This small sound is her call   obi

Unwinding its path
Silk falling   as centuries pass

This is a gloved hand over a woman's mouth
Coat rip   suitcase spilling

Hair comb   dress   keys
A ring of keys

Which peck the planked ground
Unwelcome flock

Do not step where he hates the song
This small sound is her call   scarf

Plucked from the neck
Silk falling   as centuries pass

This is the board that is sparrow
This is the board that is nightingale

THE LADY OF OPLONTIS RECEIVES A CAT SCAN

A victim of the A.D. 79 eruption of Mt. Vesuvius receives medical attention

Chariot grooves point the direction
Lady O was headed, bracelets snaking
up her arm, purse chiming with change.

Forensic filament, she's ours
for the keeping now. Watch how lovely,
like an heirloom slipping into a lake,

her head sinks into our cold pillows.
We'll unlatch the canopy her body
cut out, count her cavities,

her childbearing years.
Perhaps we've seen her before—
running for the bus, coat shrugging

like a chiton from her arms,
or the waitress whose perfect handling
of orders makes her perfectly forgettable.

The hands we know, but not the face,
blurred by our precipitous hungers.
Loaves in the oven, mouths to fill—

always some everyday stifle, reason
to get back. Sulfur mingles with a town's
fish scent and no one notices.

The heat not unbearable,
but the air dry. She passed the gate,
kept walking. The scanner's eye

promises us her Promethean
return. The lab tech's coat, brushing
her hips, conducts a shock.

She slowed her step to read the Vesuvian
sky. Her thirst a disrupted thought,
mouth cast into a final O.

QUICK, *1821*
New England, on legislation defining the development of a human soul

And on the 28th day

no blood had come as written on the papyrus.
As written on the acacia leaf. As written on the forbidden.
There were times when my master's arms were my stockade.
His white hands, cupped in prayer, trembled

about my breasts as if trying to contain water.
Mistress Mary, have mercy. When he doused the fire,
I did not wilt but grasped the meaning of my anatomy—
its fluctuations, its gluttony. I cannot help

what has been taught me. There is a fleshy flame
quickening below my apron. Like the flood,
a male soul takes just 40 days. Yet, if it be female,
I have time. Send your miracle of tea stains.

Mother Mary, have mercy. Your halo shames,
your blue eyes forecast my lie. In your hands—
pomegranate, hook & buttonweed. The babe
suckling at your breast looks to be a grown man.

The Virgins of Murano

Gatherer, marver, cutter of necks,
the mustached Gabriel burns
with the chemistry of glass.

November's a busy month:
ten haloed forms reflect the furnace
tongue. In the kiln their corsets

flicker and glow, votive.
Lost sailors sifted heat-hard beads
from a campfire's cold bed

and brought the currency north.
He's trapped in the substance, a flaw
in glass, watching through slats

as the Murano girls rush to meet
the ships at port. He molds each sheer
shackle into porthole lace, taps

the hem free, melds the cullet
into glory hole. Part water,
part sand, she is the island's unravel.

He'd throw the pretty thing—
milk bottle, flask—if she weren't filled
with his exhale. Vitrified vessel,

she'll export his breath as he remains
at the crucible, repeating the secret
he never chose to know.

Brown

Ann Nisei says:
Camp newlyweds, hang brown
curtains for privacy, to brighten the barracks
into home....

Sugar beet pyramids,
the Minidoka sky smeared by dust storm.
The pan of the panhandle state.
A field worker's tan lines.

Eel on a slab of rice.
Buckwheat tea, milk-lightened, to soothe the bitterness.

The cracks in my hands where dirt settled:
not once, but twice
& the empty fairgrounds' knee-deep mud
where we waited for the train
that dragged me back.

The fields of childhood.

Our shadows in the fields,
an asymmetrical line of three girls, kneeling.
Strawberry baskets, nearly filled.

Along the tracks: a smashed violin case,
a Nippon grandfather clock, tumbleweed,
then heaps of potatoes & beets—
those buried crops.

The shoes of the camp woman crushed by a tractor.
The beets she held.

Jackson street's cable cars.
His skin against mine.

The uniform of the non-No-No boys
& the herons woven in my marriage kimono
against a minty swamp.

...for an artful & inexpensive accent
pin-up etchings, set out a flat bowl, introduce just a dash of color.

Leave the froufrou & pastel
to the others. Show your husband you're smart
& bold—paint one wall a deep, warm chocolate.

Refinery smoke & tobacco stains.
The wooden chair where my husband sat before he enlisted.

The gunnysacks we lay across the bare floor.
My honeymoon. My trousseau.

Lot, *2003*
Oregon, on a clinic protest

I am chained to a crying boy

whose coat is lettered LIFE. Mother tells me
of the gravel nights she searched for me in the headlights—
I wasn't born yet & died, swaddled in her hands
like a cat's heart. I was a red jewel

she buried beside the road. She calls me Miracle,
child of second chance. As my legs & seat
go numb, I try to remember why I chose
to be born again. When the cars swerve too close,

I take hold of the boy's wet thumb & sing
something God will recognize. Soon I'll grow breasts
& eggs that bleed out payment for the sins
of the girls lost as mother once was. They drive

from here onto desolate roads. For now, I wear layers
to hide my knots. Tonight my face will appear on TV.
I am the brown-haired girl, rocking a red-dyed
doll. Our eyes closed, praying to be found.

Leuna Fields
Angola, Africa

The grasses quickly forget their slaughter,
                        the seasons dressing them bright
            as a girl in a cotton dress.

    They blossom, they leaf, they entice.

            At sunrise, the left behind lock
their orphans safe into the train station shell,
                        listening for the ghosts

    reborn light-footed in the clover—

Little Moses who crawled into the reeds
                        to eat from the exotic bowl
            or the leathered couple forever stooped

    to finger a dried sycamore.

            They gather their limbs for warmth.
Each phantom bone reaches into the land's
                        full trap, never wanting again.

    They grow into oak, into hemlock, into fern.

Each day the living clear a path further
                        through the sulfur stars. Soon they will arrive
            away from here and their lost parties.

    Already they see through fewer eyes.

            Once they walked barefoot. Now they wear
a foot in their shoe, an arm in their sleeve.
                        Their bodies are stools they rest upon.

    They take them off to dream at night.

Hand mit Ringen

from Bertha Roentgen's hand X-ray

This is my bone bound with your ring.

Hinged in brevity my hand fans,
My skin is a requiem. Remember me 1896.
In the gesture I beckon:

Enter my ghost's corridor & shipwreck.
Crawl between the piping of my satin casket.
Here are the keys dangling from my pelvis—

Touch my skeleton.

This is the way into my darkness
Where I inhume the whalebone beneath
The window & nestle into the pine box bed

To shroud myself with the less
Gentle sex. Slamming doors, letting the wind
Blow through my legs. Skull & cross-

Bone mad. Here, I vanish

Only to arrive days later, disheveled.
The X-ray's predilection for cells
Out of place suits me. This debridement

Is better than the old cinch & buttress.
Exhume my first wanton hologram:
The rat's nest & glass eye, my ten charred nails.

I am radiant.

"Pomona" is for Paula McLain.

"Second Hand" is for Laurel Minter.

"Graft": Section epigraphs are taken from *The Expert Gardener: or, A treatise containing certaine necessary, secret, and ordinary knowledges in grafting and gardening…faithfully collected out of sundry Dutch and French authors* printed by Richard Herne, 1640. The Marquis De Sade's letters were found in *At Home with the Marquis De Sade: A Life* by Fancine Du Plessix Gray, 1998.

"The Bookbinder": Mary Reynolds lived as an expatriate and artisan bookbinder in Paris following World War I. Using found objects to illustrate the writers' dadaist puns, she bound collections by Paul Eluard and Jean Cocteau among others. She and Marcel Duchamp were intimates and collaborators for more than twenty years. During World War II she remained in Paris to work in the French Resistance; following the war, she applied for work in the United States Secret Service. Her collection is housed at The Art Institute of Chicago. The biographical facts informing this poem were mostly found in "Warm Ashes: The Life and Career of Mary Reynolds" by Susan Glover Godlewski in *The Art Institute of Chicago Museum Studies*, 22, no. 2, 1996.

"Time Capsule" is for Michael Wilson.

"Foul, *600*"; "Clouds, *1677*"; "Quick, *1821*"; and "Lot, *2003*": The historical references presented in these poems were taken from a time line on reproduction.

"Brown": The poem references "Ann Nisei Says," a lady's advice column for women detained in the Japanese-American internment camps, in specific "A Barrack Home for Newlyweds in Relocation Centers" in *Pacific Citizen*, 15, no. 28 (December 10, 1942).

"Rehearsing Death": The title refers to an ancient term for asthma as described by Seneca. The poem's imagery reflects artworks by Emma Hauck and Marie Lieb in *Beyond Reason: Art and Psychosis, Works from the Prinzhorn Collection*, 1996 and Margaret Meehan's "The Burden of Memory."

"The Virgins of Murano": To protect Italy's monopoly on glass production in the 16th century, the State Inquisition forbade Murano Island glassmakers from leaving the island.

"Luena Fields": This poem speaks to the atrocities inflicted by land mines and was informed by the photography of Don Doll, S.J.

"Hand mit Ringen": At the turn of the century it became popular for a young woman to give her beloved an x-ray image of her hand wearing a ring he had given her. Fragments of text are taken from *Screening the Body: Tracing Medicine's Visual Culture* by Lisa Cartwright, 1995.

ABOUT THE AUTHOR

Glori Simmons is the recipient of several poetry prizes including the Poetry Society of America's Alice Fay Di Castagnola Award and Lucille Medwick Memorial Award. Her poetry has been published in the *Beloit Poetry Journal*, *Quarterly West*, and *Black Warrior Review*, among others. Originally from the Northwest, she currently lives in San Francisco.